Portrait of

WASHINGTON

Portrait of America Series

PORTRAIT OF
WASHINGTON

Photography by John Marshall

Text by Ruth Kirk

GRAPHIC ARTS CENTER PUBLISHING™

WASHINGTON

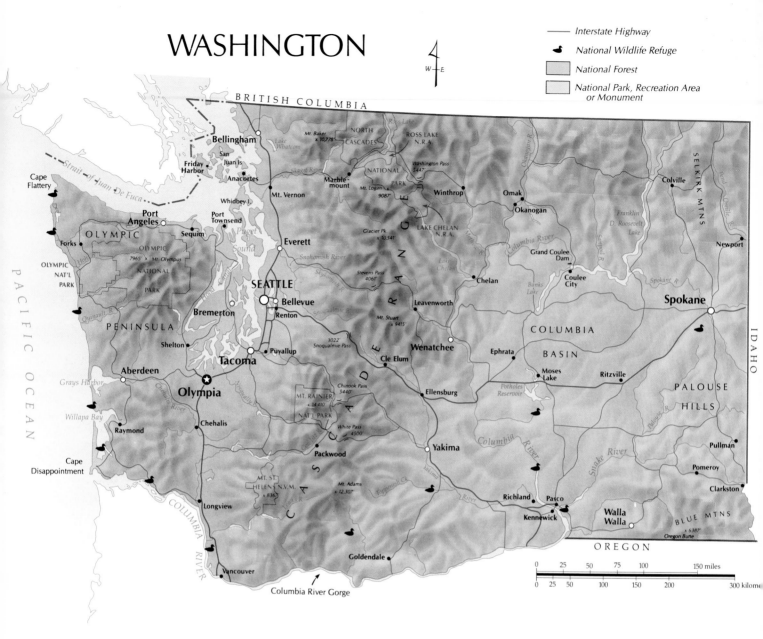

Interstate Highway
National Wildlife Refuge
National Forest
National Park, Recreation Area or Monument

International Standard Book Number 1-55868-154-X
Library of Congress Catalog Number 93-70508
© MCMXCIII by Graphic Arts Center Publishing Company
P.O. Box 10306 • Portland, Oregon 97210
503/226-2402
No part of this book may be reproduced by any
means without the permission of the publisher.
President • Charles M. Hopkins
Editor-in-Chief • Douglas A. Pfeiffer
Managing Editor • Jean Andrews
Production Manager • Richard L. Owsiany
Typographer • Harrison Typesetting, Inc.
Color Separations • Agency Litho
Printing • Moore Lithograph, Inc.
Binding • Lincoln & Allen
Printed in the United States of America
Second Printing

■ *Front cover photograph:* Its base some ten miles wide, 14,411-foot Mount Rainier encompasses thirty-five square miles of glaciers. ■ *Frontispiece:* A hydropower plant has generated electricity at 268-foot Snoqualmie Falls since 1898. ■ *Above:* Summer winds make Long Beach an ideal site for the International Kite Festival.

■ *Left:* Air trapped under ice creates intricate patterns when Icicle Creek's flow drops during a cold snap. ■ *Above:* In true Western tradition, Blue Mountain cowboys ride the high country near Dayton, searching for strays as winter approaches. ■ *Overleaf:* At 7,965 feet, Mount Olympus—with ice up to nine hundred feet deep on its six glaciers—is the highest peak in the Olympic Mountains.

THE RIGHT WASHINGTON
by Ruth Kirk

THE WEST SIDE. To me, this is not the "other" Washington that is mentioned in tourism ads as an oblique reference to Washington, D.C. This is the "right" Washington.

I sit musing aboard our small sloop, *Taku*. We are close to the urban throb of today's cities, yet the boat is no more than a tiny dot on a blue and green tapestry of sea and forest. By chance, this quiet southern Puget Sound cove where we ride at anchor is near where Lieutenants Peter Puget and William Whidbey camped—in "a perfect deluge of rain"—the second night out from *Discovery,* the ship commanded by the great British mariner, Captain George Vancouver. That was two centuries ago. Puget and Whidbey were in open longboats powered by oarsmen. Their task, according to a memo from Vancouver to Puget, was to "Survey the Shore."

Two decades later, fur traders began to crisscross the territory. Three decades after that, Lieutenant Charles Wilkes, of the U.S. Navy, surveyed Puget Sound and recognized its value along a coast with no other faintly comparable break from San Francisco to Vancouver Island (indeed, no other large indentation except for Gray's Harbor). Wilkes urged sovereignty over these inland waters, a recommendation that contributed to American insistence on the 49th parallel as the boundary between the United States and Canada.

Britain also wanted Puget Sound—and the entire territory north of the Columbia River—but trade along the coast to Alaska was their top priority. What later became Washington could be sacrificed. Thus, in 1846, mapmakers inked in today's international line.

While sailing, my husband, Louis, and I have felt the continuity between those beginnings and the present. We have reveled in broad waterways, tall trees, and snow-capped mountains. Houses intermix, but—from the water—rarely predominate. Southern Puget Sound permits an illusion of timelessness. Two humpback whales are reported this summer, although we have not seen them. Our wildlife coup has been a bald eagle, which we watched as it swooped to the water and rose with a silvery salmon clutched in its talons.

A rural quality lingers along the entire western shore of Puget Sound, from Olympia to Port Townsend; along much of the eastern shore, only Seattle's blocky, black, seventy-six-story Columbia Center jutting above the horizon breaks the spell. Without it, you would have little inkling of a city's proximity. An evening excursion from Seattle to Blake Island can still include a stroll along grassy shores and pristine beaches frequented by deer, then a salmon dinner prepared and served by Native Americans.

Left: Quileute Indians, whose ancestors pursued fish and sea mammals in canoes, fish for smelt on the Olympic coast.

Lieutenants Puget and Whidbey met Natives a few miles north of where we now are anchored. The explorers had started to seine a creek mouth for fish, but they quit when Salish canoes entered the cove. The new arrivals were clearly displeased. The Englishmen moved on before camping.

In the 1960s, while Louis served as ranger-naturalist at Olympic National Park, we watched Quileute men at La Push and the mouth of the Hoh River make cedar dugout canoes. Charlie Howeattle and Ted Hudson would rough out canoe blanks from split-cedar logs using chain saws, then switch to hand tools. These included a D-adze with a whalebone handle and a blade from a Hudson's Bay Company trade axe. Result? Canoes to be fitted with outboard motors and used for gillnetting salmon.

The old-time canoemakers are gone, but descendants in a dozen western Washington tribes carved cedar canoes as part of the 1989 statehood Centennial celebration. They used logs obtained through the National Forest Service and, on the Peninsula, felled by the state Department of Natural Resources, and delivered by the National Park Service.

Such craft were fifty feet long and six feet wide. They plied this state's coastline, carrying villagers forty in a canoe to potlatches (ceremonial occasions fundamental to Northwest Coast Indian culture) or—two canoes lashed together as a catamaran—moving families and household goods from one site to another. Canoes also took men onto the open ocean to hunt whales and fur seals and sea otters, and to fish for halibut and salmon. "We were all the time going places in canoes," Ada Markishtum, an aging Makah woman, told me, when I visited her to learn to make cedar-bark baskets. "Even we children knew how to sit still." She reminisced about waiting for favorable winds and tides, then sailing and paddling across the Strait of Juan de Fuca with her grandmother to trade baskets for blankets and other goods at the Hudson's Bay Company in Victoria, British Columbia.

Today's Native Americans still travel widely. I think, for example, of Makah friends who drove two hundred miles from their Neah Bay reservation to Olympia to officially open an exhibit of early-day tribal photographs. As a prelude, they danced on the gray marble floor of the Capitol rotunda. Their drumbeats and songs manifested the new vigor sweeping Washington's Native community.

A velvet rope—which usually surrounds the golden seal in the middle of the floor—had been removed, and there the masked dancers whirled. The scarlet "button blankets" they wore flared dramatically to display cutouts of Thunderbird and Whale and Wolf appliqued in black. Sequins as well as buttons now highlight these figures. Native Americans are adaptable. How else could they survive?

The Olympic Mountains rim the western horizon most of this day of sailing. A jumble of peaks not topping eight thousand feet in elevation, they nonetheless are whitened by some fifty glaciers. Clouds from the Pacific replenish the ice. Chilled while sweeping upward, droplets turn to crystals, then fall as a blanket of white. For five years we lived on the Olympic Peninsula. I still feel that of all the "right" places in this state, the Peninsula just may be best. Its towns are humane in scale—perhaps to the regret of boosters.

Forks and Aberdeen/Hoquiam, on the west side, are hard hit by recent slowdowns in the forest products industry. Near-term recovery is problematical owing to the depletion of trees to cut. Port Townsend, at the northeast tip of the Peninsula has had enthusiasm and Victorian mansions, but its downtown buildings have always stayed half empty. Once, the tall masts of late-1800s ships lined wharves, and entrepreneurs fostered hope of a link to the transcontinental railroad. But shipping moved on, and rails never came.

Sequim now has several stoplights and a constant influx of retirees who enjoy the drier weather in the "rain shadow" of the Olympic Mountains. Nearby Port Angeles, largest of the Peninsula's towns, has a population of about twenty thousand; it takes fifteen minutes to drive kitty-corner across town. For a city interlude, you can board the ferry to Victoria, British Columbia (one and a half hours away), or go to Seattle (two hours by road plus bridge plus ferry).

Two roads and a host of trails lead to the subalpine meadows of the Olympics where purple lupine and scarlet paintbrush and golden arnica and a burst of other flowers brighten entire hillsides. Marmots—furry woodchucks—feed on the flowers, sitting on their haunches and pulling the blossoms to their mouths with their forepaws. The marmots tunnel up through snow to begin active life after a winter of hibernation; then curl back underground when the fall vegetation scents the air with the aroma of natural silage.

While in the mountains, I think they are my favorite part of the Peninsula. Then we hike the wilderness coast, and I am sure the beach is my primary love. *I've been lazy*, reads a note in my journal while camped at Point of Arches, the northern-most Olympic National Park beach:

Last night's darkness didn't begin until after 10:30, and it never amounted to much. I slept outside the tent beside a drift log, head toward the jagged near-shore islets and arches that make this beach the most wondrous in the state. Each time I turned, I could check the tide and the night sky's alteration between clouds and stars.

Low tide—a minus 1.4 feet—came at 5:00 A.M. I should have gone with Louis to the tidepools. Instead, at 8:00, the breakfast fire still holds me, its warmth contrasting with the gray chill of the morning. I forgot to bring my favorite camera lens, and that oversight serves as excuse for laziness. We moderns seem to suffer guilt when we fail to "collect" our experiences.

Aboard *Taku* now, I think of the tidepools. I should have looked with eyes, if not with camera: water clear, bottoms bejeweled with pink coralline seaweed and jade-green anemones. But I think too of a friend who said that tidepools seem frightening. "It's the ruthlessness. A crab or something falls into an anemone and Whomp! That's the end."

Today, Louis and I rowed ashore and walked paths on Hartstene Island. There, Douglas fir grow three feet in diameter, a respectable forest though previously logged. Trees are not a crop "just like corn." We have cut and replanted and cut again, but we will not be able to keep on doing so in the same way. Our existing "harvest" techniques violate too many intricate linkages between organisms.

Western Washington forests renew themselves through small and patchy disasters, not wholesale wipeouts. A raging stream pouring rocks and mud down a sidehill or a blow-down toppling a section of forest—even the uprooting of one tree, which churns the soil and opens the canopy to sunlight. These are the events that perpetuate the green diversity of forests west of the Cascade Mountains. In the stands planted after clear-cutting, sheer density of sapling growth absorbs available light and produces an underlying wasteland of brown needles and infertile shadow that lasts for decades.

A natural forest differs greatly. Plants carpet its floor so densely that "nurselogs" offer seedlings a valuable perch. Logs also deliver ready-made nutrients when they fall, and accumulate still more as they decay. World-renowned ecologist Jerry Franklin speaks of the need to manage deadwood as deliberately as has been true of sawlogs. "A tree does all kinds of good things after it dies," he says. "Its ecological role is as great as while it was alive."

Burning the debris left from logging, a common practice that turns autumn skies murky, squanders potential. It volatilizes nitrogen in woody tissues and short-circuits intricate relationships. Regarding fallen trees as "over mature" and useless ignores their after-death role, for down-trees remain an important part of the forest community. What actually happens when a tree falls is this: the trunk is recruited to the forest floor ("recruitment" is a term used by forest ecologists). Beetles and nematodes and a great host of other organisms soon invade the log, bringing with them yeasts and the spores of fungi. These initiate a whole new cycle of nutrient build-up. "There actually are more living cells in a well-rotted log than there were while it stood as part of a living tree," Jerry points out.

Bacteria capable of drawing nitrogen from the air enter through the beetles' galleries. Some fungi arriving through those portals have enzyme systems that decompose a range of complex woody compounds. Some produce antibiotics, which suppress certain bacteria. Others give off volatiles that inhibit specific organisms and stimulate others. Certain fungi, thriving only on the roots of living plants, improve their hosts' ability to draw nutrients and moisture from the soil. Hemlock seedlings barely survive until this mutually beneficial relationship is established; their growth depends on the association with fungus.

When you walk beneath trees two hundred feet tall and as much as a thousand years old—or visit the red-cedar grove on Long Island in Willapa Bay, perpetuated without major disturbance for some four thousand years—you *look* at more than you *see*. A forest is a community; trees are one part of the whole.

For millennia, forest and water set the stage for human life in this wet west side of Washington. Then newcomers usurped land from Indians, bringing new aspirations and habits. Settlement accelerated in the late 1840s, after the boundary issue was settled with England. In the 1870s and 1890s, the nation endured depressions, partly owing to the new industrialization. As if in response, Washingtonians experimented with various reforms, including half-a-dozen idealistic settlements scattered around Puget Sound.

Best known of these was the community of Home, situated at the cove where I now sit on the bow of *Taku* enjoying the alpenglow on Mount Rainier, fifty miles to the east. Home was free-spirited. Its successive newspapers espoused "radical" convictions, urging that women should be allowed to vote; that religion should not be coerced; and that love between men and women ought to be a matter of choice, not law. Furthermore, both speakers and writers championed the belief that "security is not to be promoted by stifling the voice of discontent, but by removing its cause."

Such advocacies cost the paper its mailing privileges and triggered the closure of Home's post office in 1902. Trouble climaxed ten years later when a Tacoma jury convicted Home residents of swimming nude. The town's editor printed a commentary titled "prudes *versus* nudes"—and went to jail for two months.

Today, back-to-the-land movements readily take root in backwoods corners, and even in cities, an awareness of frontier lingers. Washington closets hold ski boots, hiking boots, and hip boots; and anyone blessed with a low enough REI number is likely to mention it as a form of upmanship. Louis and I have Number 6275, which is moderately prestigious. It identifies us as old-timers at Recreational Equipment, Inc., the co-op supplier of outdoor equipment that began in Seattle in 1938 and today has numerous far-flung branches. We joined REI in 1952.

King County, with one-third of the state's population, now dickers over shipping its trash somewhere to a rural county, and state fisheries officials contemplate the wisdom of upriver rides for salmon trying to spawn in drought-lowered waters. Nuclear submarines berth near Bremerton. Boeing planes circle the globe. Sea-Tac airport—which was new when we first came to the state—must be augmented.

Bellevue—where a whaling fleet used to tie up for the winter—now bristles with glassy high-rises that look like Newport Beach, California, somehow transplanted in the north. Yet in spite of all this, both *yuppies* and folks in the boondocks dig clams, cut firewood, and fill freezers with venison and wild huckleberries.

My friend Dave Pugh, former Chief of Interpretation for the northwest region of the National Park Service, moved here from the San Francisco Bay area. He points out that much of the sense of space within the Puget Sound megalopolis derives from the merciful screening effect of vegetation. "Cut the trees and we'd all be surprised at how crowded it actually is," he says. I suppose he is right. But—call it youthful confidence or call it mature environmental awareness—we western Washingtonians expect to have both scenery and cities. We belong to the 1990s, but we also rejoice in our 1790s scenery.

Lieutenants Puget and Whidbey would notice scattered lights if they were to again spend a night near this cove, but they would also still be able to recognize the shore. Time rests gently throughout most of the Puget Sound lowlands and river valleys.

THE MOUNTAIN SPINE. Louis and I moved to Mount Rainier in the early 1950s, transferred by the National Park Service from Death Valley and the tall cactus country of the borderlands near Mexico. The van driver who brought our goods said, "You've moved from the ridiculous to the sublime."

And sublime it was—although for a full two weeks the mountain stayed hidden within the clouds, and even where to look for it puzzled me. Our kids, ages five and seven, immediately set out exploring and soon reported back astonished: "There's *nothing* poisonous here." No rattlesnakes or scorpions, no cactus thorns. Nonetheless, at first I worried that the boys might get lost while playing in the forest. In the desert, no vegetation had blocked their view back to the house.

Funny things happened. A man once came to the ranger station and asked to borrow a skillet. When I asked if they had forgotten theirs, he answered, "No. We have it but the campfire would get it dirty." Once, tourists pressed their noses against our windows and exclaimed: "Look. There are people in there!" And a woman getting off a bus asked to use our bathroom because she would feel embarrassed to be seen walking to the public rest rooms.

Raccoons and spotted skunks lived under the floor of the house and sometimes fought, a bit odorous for us all. Bats roosted in the wall of our bedroom, and the first couple of nights, Louis thought their odd sounds were me snoring—and I thought they were him snoring. Bears raided the garbage can. One was experienced enough to sit beside the can, straddle it with his hind legs, then tip it gently and slide off the lid. That avoided the clatter he had learned would bring someone to shoo him away.

For a while, a young buck deer tried to join the family. Someone (wrongly) must have taken him from the wild as a fawn, then brought him back when antlers started to appear. More acquainted with people than with other deer, the buck would come onto the porch and whine on cold, rainy days. He enjoyed riding in the cab of the snowplow and tried repeatedly to board the school bus. Twice, he managed to get on the bus, but he ate sandwiches out of lunch bags and turned himself from a novelty into an enemy.

Next he walked into the office and ate forms used to account for park entrance fees. That was the end. He was moved to fenced land near Tacoma, an explosives manufacturing site that was a fur-trading post in the 1800s and, now, is Northwest Landing, a planned community developed by Weyerhaeuser Real Estate Company. Soon we heard that workmen there were finding lunch bags ripped open, and we knew someone else had left a door open.

Mount Rainier is the tallest of Washington's many peaks. To check its height, surveyors in 1988 carried equipment to the summit for a remeasurement. They recorded signals from satellites, the first use of modern celestial technology for assessing a terrestrial peak. Their results—14,411 feet, accurate within inches—were released during the state's Centennial celebration, eighty years after the first measurement. That first measurement, in 1909, placed the height at 14,150 feet. Four years later, this was changed to 14,408. Then in 1956, the mountain "grew" an additional two feet to 14,410. More telling, however, than the changing figures is that, although Mount Rainier ranks fifth in height among the peaks of the lower forty-eight states, it is the highest above its immediate base. Longmire's elevation is only 2,760 feet, whereas the champion peak, Mount Whitney, California (14,495 feet above sea level) and the soaring peaks of the Colorado Rockies start from land already a mile high.

We lived at Rainier when the 1956 measurement was made. It involved lifting U.S. Geological Survey men and triangulation equipment to the summit by helicopter. The pilot did not want to go; the thin air at such an extreme elevation posed a real hazard for a helicopter. He insisted the doors be taken off and the battery removed after he started the rotor—anything to lighten the load. Then he carried surveyors and equipment up, and later brought the men down. But he refused to go back for the equipment.

Consequently, my husband and another ranger climbed the mountain to bring off the gear and install a new benchmark. I got to go along. On our backs, we carried cement and also gasoline to use as fuel for melting ice, which was needed to mix the cement into concrete for use around the benchmark. In my journal, I noted:

At 1:00 A.M. we left Camp Muir, the traditional ten-thousand-foot base camp for summit climbs. No moon, so we used headlamps. I was tired, and moving through the darkness seemed like having on a huge hat with the brim hanging down.

Before dawn, the "blinders" effect started to ease. Irregularities in the snow surface cast enough shadow to give texture to the otherwise black world. Then a faintly bright streak lined the eastern horizon. Next— at last—pink light hit the summit and slid down the glacier to warm us. It seemed awfully long in coming.

The new benchmark is located at the high point along the northern rim of the summit crater. Just inside the rim, the ground is free of snow and ice. In fact, it's too hot to sit on.

We Washingtonians feel a connection with the mountain spine dividing us into east and west. We see our peaks while going about daily rounds. The Wenatchee Mountains rise beyond the wheat fields of the Waterville Plateau. Mount Adams shows from Yakima. Mount Rainier dots the horizon as you drive toward Ellensburg from Vantage, and it looms huge as you roll along I-5 between Seattle and Olympia. Mount Baker and the North Cascades backdrop tulip fields of the Skagit River delta. And of course there is Mount St. Helens. We almost hoped it would erupt—until it did so and became a two-year nuisance. St. Helens still evokes the question, Where were you when the mountain blew?

At our home in Tacoma, the May 18, 1980, eruption did little except turn the eastern sky murky and fill television screens with images of the Toutle River pouring water from suddenly melted glaciers against the I-5 bridge. Later, lesser eruptions dusted our petunias with ash and turned my computer keyboard gritty when I forgot to cover it.

Even eastern Washingtonians who lived through the darkness-at-noon trauma and the heavy shoveling of fallout from the initial eruption grew weary from what seemed like endless small effects. "I'm so tired of sand between my toes when the nearest beach is two hundred miles away," a woman living in the Ahtanum Valley near Yakima told us. "Why do geologists speak of volcanic *ash*? It's *sand*."

I have read that the May 18 eruption equaled the force of thirty atom bombs like the one dropped at Hiroshima; also that it equated with five hundred atom bombs. Either way, mighty though it was, the Mount St. Helens blast was puny, even among other Northwest volcanic eruptions. Mount Mazama, Oregon, ejected nine and one-half cubic miles of debris when it formed Crater Lake and dusted Washington with ash nearly seven thousand years ago. Archaeologists readily recognize this ash within excavation walls and use it as a time marker: anything lying undisturbed above the ash is more recent than the eruption; anything below it is older.

They also use ash from previous St. Helens eruptions. The most recent major eruption spewed barely one-quarter cubic mile of ejecta—useful for future archaeologists, but quite modest compared to Mount Mazama's greatest blast.

Perhaps what the 1980 eruption did above all else was remind us that "dormant" is not "dead." Our human time scale, imbued with an awareness of individual life spans, gives a poor sense of nature's schedules. St. Helens had not erupted for a century. To most of us, but not to scientists, that had seemed to lessen the probability of eruption. Not so.

My favorite place to marvel at the shaping of mountains is Harts Pass, above the town of Winthrop (known now for its Hollywood-frontier atmosphere, but actually a late 1800s supply point for ranchers and miners). I like the Harts Pass Road—narrow, rough, and unpaved—because it claws its way into the mountains. Meet an oncoming car, and one of you must back. You hug contours rather than conquer them, as is true while driving the smooth ribbon of the North Cascades Highway.

Beyond 6,197-foot Harts Pass, the highest point in the state reached by road, a fire lookout tops Slate Peak. From it, you gaze southeast toward peaks gouged into fangs by glacier ice. The Needles and Liberty Bell tower above the North Cascades Highway. Forty-six miles westward is Mount Baker. North is the Pasayten Wilderness. You might feel guilty for having won experience of such *mountain-ness* with tires instead of boots, were it not for the sheer exhilaration of beholding such beauty.

I marvel at the indomitable spirit of miners who penetrated this realm, which is more vertical than horizontal. In the 1890s, they used horses to pack in a steam-powered stampmill; then they packed out gold for shipment down the Columbia. In the 1900s, they upgraded the old horse trail into a road wide enough for trucks with eighteen inches cut from their axles. Winter contact with the outside world was by dogsled, a scheduled service that brought in mail, supplies, and a motion picture, and took out mail and gold.

The *Okanogan Heritage*, a historical quarterly, printed a 1935 letter from a miner at Azurite Mine to his wife:

We had a long cold spell, 29 below and froze our water pipe up and we have to carry our water from the creek up hill through the deep snow. . . . It turned warm and started to snow. I never saw anything like it—seven feet in two days. It then started to rain and poured down for three days. The old snow was packed hard and conditions were just right for snowslides.

They started at once and hell was popping for five days. There was hardly a five-minute interval that you couldn't see a slide running in the daytime or hear one roar at night. Some of the big ones filled the air with snow so you could hardly see.

Buildings got knocked down; part of the sawmill caved in from snow load. An avalanche buried the bull cook, but rescuers dug him free. "We are having wonderful, mild clear weather now," the letter concludes, "but when the next heavy snow comes there will be some nervous men here."

Mining began in the Okanogan Cascades in the 1860s when prospectors, who had rushed to the gold boom along British Columbia's Fraser River, returned empty-handed. Some say that in 1846, surveyors determining the international boundary noticed gold in the Similkameen River.

Early claims were for placer gold washed down from the mountains. It settled in streams and rivers in shiny flecks and nuggets that miners collected by swirling water in pans or "rockers," boxes filled with gravel and water, then tilted back and forth to catch gold against built-in baffles. White men often worked such claims and moved on. Chinese miners then took over, sometimes succeeding where get-rich-quick impulses had failed. Ditches dug to divert water for gold operations also irrigated vegetable gardens, the first of the systems that now carry water to orchards and fields.

Hardrock mining came next. Its leftovers still dot the mountains, for following veins into the earth itself required machinery, which required a capital outlay undreamed of by placer miners. That investment of capital, in turn, offered its own possibilities of wealth—with or without ore.

At the Monte Cristo mine (up the Stillaguamish drainage from Everett), the J. D. Rockefeller syndicate invested three million dollars and got a return on its money. Conversely, near Loomis, the Palmer Mountain Tunnel and Power Company floated stock, blasted a mile-long tunnel, and built a concentrating mill. Its many windows neither lit nor ventilated the conversion of ore into matte, however; all that came of the mill was the tar and feathering of a reporter who wrote about its assured profit and jobs.

Another monument to hope, or folly, is the "China Wall." Jonathan Bourne, Jr., arrived in the Northwest in 1878. Shipwrecked off Formosa, he had met a sea captain who was bringing Chinese laborers to the Northwest, a virtual slave trade dealing in human cargo. Bourne took passage from Hong Kong to Portland, passed the Oregon bar, then spent his energy organizing mining ventures and dabbling in politics rather than practicing law. With investment money from fellow members of Portland's aristocratic Arlington Club, he bought claims south of Conconully and organized a mining company named for the club. There he built the foundation for a huge mill: the China Wall.

One summer, we turned off the Loop Loop Pass Road to find the mill site. We wound up a narrow valley, unsure of the precise location but knowing what to watch for. The actualities surprised us. Walls, nearly obscured by Douglas fir and larch, would be easy to pass without noticing, though one section bulks fully thirty feet high and eighty feet long. No Chinese were associated with Bourne's company; the nickname, "China Wall," comes from its built-for-eternity character. Chris Starzman, a stonemason, directed the work. Among those under him were Antoine Ritchie, a Frenchman from Canada who lived in the valley nearby (the ruins of his cabin still stand); John Bawlf, a Civil War veteran who had crossed the Great Plains to Coulee City by wagon train; and Robert Saltmarsh, a wheat farmer from Almira who worked on the wall to earn cash.

Somehow Starzman got these and other equally inexperienced men to build walls fit for an imperial palace. Three to four feet thick, corners of granite blocks, the walls are aesthetically and functionally perfect—or would have been functional had the mill been finished. But it was not. Freighters brought equipment, including two three-ton boilers, into the little valley, a feat in itself; tens of thousands of bricks were delivered; and huge squared timbers were hewn. But fate decreed that no complete superstructure should rise from the magnificent foundation. Bourne began work on the mill in August 1889, ordered a stop in May 1890. His Arlington Club investors had tired of pouring money into the ground, getting none back out.

Obviously, all who live among mountains experience their moods, but in Washington, the lowlanders also are affected. We watch the peaks dress and undress seasonally and know that the world is white as well as blue and green. Paradise, a mile-high shoulder of Mount Rainier, has logged a record snowfall of 1,027 inches, a blanket so deep that winter access to backcountry cabins comes only by digging *down* to second-story windows. Often well into July, guests enter Paradise Inn via snow tunnel.

By then, avalanche lilies are heralding a parade of bloom so wondrous that if rainbows were on the ground instead of among the clouds, alpine meadows would surely be their home. Winter flakes, of course, restore the mountains' white robe. Skiers rejoice. Ours is more than a poetic passion for mountains. We actively pursue their delights.

EASTERN WASHINGTON. Spokane is well nicknamed the Queen City of the Inland Empire. Travel through, and little of the charm is apparent. Pause, and you find it.

"Architecture offers a way to get a handle on Spokane," said Scott Brooks-Miller, once Historic Preservation Officer for the city. Then he outlined a tour ranging from buildings in the shape of milk bottles (intended as ice cream parlors) and an automotive repair garage (with an entry that looks like a 1930s car radiator) to storybook mansions in Browne's Addition and on South Hill.

Young and knowledgeable, Brooks-Miller explained: "Eastern Washington has had three centers: Walla Walla, Colfax, and Spokane. Today, Walla Walla has the state penitentiary and the U.S. Army Corps of Engineers. Colfax

has a thousand people more than it did in 1890. And Spokane is where everybody goes—for everything.

"A rail connection to the east came here in 1881 and, about the same time, hardrock miners found first gold, then silver, copper, and lead. That combination of trains and mines gave Spokane its start as an economic center extending from British Columbia and over into Montana clear down to the Snake River and west to the Columbia." Scott then led me downtown to see the Twenty-year Buildings. He explained, "That's how long we expect construction to last these days without needing major repair." He also spoke of One-hundred-year Buildings. "They were built to last, and with modern techniques, we can keep them forever."

By the 1890s, Spokane was beyond the boomtown stage. Building styles and techniques were contemporary with the rest of the nation. Today, skywalks link these structures—the "largest and oldest skywalk network in the U.S. except for Minneapolis-St. Paul." The enclosed corridors convert most of Spokane's downtown section into a kind of mall.

Along two blocks of Stevens Street, Scott showed me buildings representing forty years of change. They stand virtually side by side, a variety of styles from the past, yet intermixed with modern construction. The earliest buildings were masonry, put up after fire leveled Spokane's mostly wooden downtown in 1889. Next, cast-iron store fronts permitted opening the street level beyond what was structurally possible with all-masonry walls, which need a thick base to support upper walls. "Cast-iron store fronts were a real advantage for shops. They let merchants display their wares to the street."

Steel construction followed the cast-iron fronts. Buildings rose higher, their walls punctured with windows. The Old National Bank Building is fifteen stories high. It gleams with white terra-cotta, a cladding that offers possibility of varied textures and shapes. On the Sherwood Building, gargoyles sit above the entry; stylized Gothic arches texture the façade. By the 1920s, Portland cement replaced lime mortar, which is vulnerable to weathering. Concrete could be poured into forms; walls could be raised by setting one preformed section on another, similar to building with stone.

"Soon after that, buildings began to lose human scale," said Scott, "but cornices and crests defined the edges, and the first couple of floors and the top floor had a lot of ornate detail. Architects still tried to catch the eye and create a give-and-take between building and beholder. Now there's more anonymity—maybe with the beginning of a return to pitched roofs and people-oriented space. Maybe we'll recycle styles, although so far architecture has never done that."

Spokane is situated north of the rich, rolling hills of the Palouse, a region blessed with deep, moisture-holding soil and spectacular production of wheat, barley, lentils, and dry peas. To be in the Palouse at harvest time is to step into a

Norman Rockwell painting updated by mechanization but with defined values remaining intact. Neighborliness. Hard work. Family. Good cheer.

We stayed at Tekoa with friends, Gene and Evelyn Fletcher, who farm twenty-seven hundred acres, some of it land Evelyn's father farmed, some of it leased. The harvest had been underway a week. When we arrived, the three Fletcher combines had just finished harvesting a barley field and were moving to a wheat field five miles away. Evelyn pinpointed their location by calling on a VHF radio, using the frequency assigned to the family's farm operation. Each combine has a radio. Each truck has one. So do the family's equipment shop, the cluster of grain storage bins, and the house. The radio helps keep the harvest moving on a nonstop basis. Just call over it to find someone to fix a breakdown, or bring replacement parts, or take a sample of newly cut grain for a moisture test. If there is more than 12 percent moisture, the elevator cannot accept it for storage.

It is 7:00 P.M. We see the combines pass the bins—three green monsters "flagged" fore and aft by trucks. We fall in behind, a parade of winking warning lights traversing a valley at ten miles per hour while the sun drops behind a ridge and suffuses us with a warm, gentle light as if coming through stained glass. We watch the combines open up the field of ripe wheat, their twenty-foot reels rotating like paddle wheels on a riverboat, chaff spewing out the rear and creating the distinctive odor of the harvest. The whole year's work hinges on these August days. Evelyn says: "The best sounds in the world are when they start the combines and when they shut them off with nobody hurt, or killed." Palouse hills are steep. Machines occasionally tip over. Furthermore, gears, conveyor belts, cutters, and augers—all constantly in motion—bring in the harvest but also pose a hazard for the weary humans tending them.

Gene says he is retired. Yet at 10 P.M. he comes home after fifteen hours in the fields, and we eat dinner. He laughs: "Oh, I work full-time during spring planting and harvest. But I don't go out to the shop anymore, or make decisions. I leave that to the boys." The "boys" are sons. Jim has a degree in oceanography and a teaching credential from Berkley. When he decided to return to farming, he studied plant pathology and microbiology. David's degree is in business administration. He returned to the Palouse after working for Dun and Bradstreet.

We talk about crops. This year the Fletchers have planted a new variety of wheat, and Gene says it looks promising. "You could hardly fit in another ten straws per acre." Other crops? "The boys played with lupine; oil from the seeds goes into margarine. It didn't grow well though, and we're too far from the processing plant anyway. Rapeseed for margarine didn't work out either. Farmers here were planting two kinds and they'd hybridize. But the cross wasn't any good."

Lentils have a happier story. Seventh-day Adventists at Farmington, south of Tekoa, grew them years ago because of their protein content; many Adventists eat no meat. Today, 90 percent of America's crop comes from this area.

I ride a combine with David harvesting lentils already swathed and left to cure. It is a dirty job. The plants grow only a foot high and the machine's lifters must run along the ground. Dust flies along with chaff. David's left hand steers; his right constantly plays a lever adjusting the height of the lifters and header. Abruptly he stops; climbs out with engine running and reel spinning; returns with a rock half the size of a Frisbee. "Hit one of these and you've trashed a $4,000 to $5,000 bar," he explains. I ride in the truck carrying the harvest to the storage bin. David's son Jonathan, a computer science major, drives. I note how intense the lentils operation is, and Jonathan agrees that his dad is more tired after a day of lentils than of wheat.

I ride with Gene cutting a wheat field. Automatic levelers keep the cab level as we contour hills, cutting, gathering, threshing, sorting, and transferring the crop from holding tank to dump truck summoned alongside by radio. Air conditioning saves broiling in the sun. Computers monitor everything from the rate of movement over the ground (averaging one mile per hour while I was aboard) to a malfunction of the chopper or conveyor or half-a-dozen other systems, or an excess of grain blowing out onto the ground. The reel turns. The ripe grain heads seem to surge into the header. We circle, empty into the truck, circle again. At dusk Gene turns on lights. Keep rolling. Get in the crop. And if your neighbor is sick, get in his, too.

Gene tells me he did not want the backbreaking work of farming as he knew it growing up. Then he adds, "But with all this mechanization, why it's fun." That "fun" involves an outlay of $160,000 in replacement cost per combine and $90,000 per tractor. Three or four weeks of harvest make or break you, depending on weather and market. In return, you get about one cent per loaf of bread. But satisfaction is deeper than economics. For Palouse farmers it comes from aesthetics of the land: hills stretched to the horizon—and you are tending them, patterning them, knowing their every light and temperature, belonging to them.

West of the Palouse, the topography roughens. Ice Age floods stripped the land to bedrock and plucked at the joints within basalt flows. The result is a maze of canyons, known as coulees, cut into the broad sagebrush plateau. Water from the Columbia Basin Project now makes much of the land green, but long before, men tried turning sweat into dryland farms. Among these optimists were—and are—the McGregors, a family whose multigeneration enterprise has evolved through a century. It began with sheep production and went on to range cattle, orchards, experimental irrigation, feed lots, meat packing, and chemical fertilizers.

In Hooper, we met Alex McGregor, author of the book, *Counting Sheep,* which chronicles family events from sheepherding days to agri-business. With a doctorate in history, Alex taught at Whitman College in Walla Walla but left to manage a division of the McGregor Company. "I wanted the business to survive as a matter of continuity, if nothing else," he says. "And since everybody in my generation was busy with other things, I switched."

We sit at the kitchen table of the comfortable two-story house where Alex was raised. He and his family recently moved to be near the main office in Colfax; previously he was commuting ninety miles a day. (Alex describes Hooper as "equally inconvenient to everywhere.") The house is one of the fourteen that constitute the entire town, along with a store building now vacant except for a ranch headquarters office, a company hotel-boarding house presently used only for community potlucks and quilting bees, a post office, operating until recently, with the original oak boxes still in place, and the old wool and sacked-wheat warehouses standing intact by the railroad track. Hooper differs from other pinprick towns in eastern Washington in that it is a company town that has been lived in by three generations of owners as well as employees. The founders were four Scots brothers who immigrated here from eastern Canada in 1882 and built the business through diligence and thrift.

"We hated to close the store," Alex says, "but when the highway moved across the valley, there weren't enough customers left. Keeping a school got to be a problem, too. Over the years, the district consolidated twelve small schools into the one at LaCrosse—and even there the high school next year will have only thirty-five kids."

McGregor Land and Livestock Company no longer raises sheep. Alex explains, "With sheep, you have to do ten things at once—everything from vaccinate the dogs to arrange for a shearing crew. Sheep are labor intensive, and agriculture has moved to mechanization." Basque herders from northern Spain cared for most Columbia Plateau flocks when Alex was growing up. In his book he tells of asking the foreman, Clemente Barber, about the health of a certain ewe belonging to a band of three thousand sheep. Barber recognized her and recited her life history beginning with abandonment as a lamb, on to the present. "Twice [last year] I pull her out of mud holes to save her," he concluded.

Remembering Barber, Alex laughs about his own first experience driving sheep as a boy. He had learned the right words from the Basques, but his inflection was wrong and the dogs absolutely refused to respond. "I sure got tired chasing those sheep by myself," he concludes.

With that, we go to the shearing shed built about 1914, so big it could shelter six thousand ewes in winter although its primary use was for lambing and shearing. Long sacks, weighing three hundred pounds apiece when full of wool,

were tamped "by jumping up and down inside the sacks." Behind the shed is a "drop wagon" much like the covered wagons used by westwardbound pioneers but equipped with rubber-tired wheels for pulling behind a pickup truck. Rows of compartments for ewes and newborn lambs line the interior. On the open range, too many lambs fell victim to bad weather or coyotes. Brought in and penned, mothers bond better with their young and give them more care. ("Sheep are smart animals, but they're smart in an unusual way," Alex says. "I'll never admit they're dumb.")

We drive through sagebrush six to eight feet tall and past bunchgrass that in a few months will have a foot of green growth. We picnic across the river from the state park at Palouse Falls (the "big falls," Alex calls them, since there are two lesser waterfalls along the Palouse River). These drop 198 feet, the water chocolate brown with soil from Palouse fields. Measurements in the winter of 1962-1963 showed twenty-two million tons of sediment going over the falls, equivalent to 160 acres of soil eighty feet deep. That was the worst year on record. Average erosion is about half of that.

"Soil loss comes from slopes that are pulverized and seeded in September. The plants sprout, then hold dormant through the winter. The ground freezes, and when rains finally come in spring, they can't soak in. We end up with a double loss: the soil erodes and the moisture we need runs off." Alex talks of fertilizers and herbicides. Aerial spraying is not as precise as ground application. The McGregors experiment with injecting fertilizer and herbicides—perhaps even combined with seed—into the ground through the previous year's stubble. That would eliminate need for tillage; and the stubble would help control erosion. Alex summarizes: "It's gratifying to be a part of agriculture's constant change—a part of history. You go out to your own blacksmith shop and see if you can affect the future."

We drive down a coulee gouged by Ice Age floods and stop at a pothole lake, where cottonwoods edge the water. Farther on, we walk to the drop-off into Palouse Canyon and gaze across the Snake River country to the Blue Mountains to the south. We revel in the scene, then return to Hooper. Alex's kids decide to take Fig Newtons to the half-dozen sheep kept as a family symbol. Perhaps it is our unfamiliar truck that sends the sheep running. Eight-year-old Ian predicts, "They'll come when Mom charms them." But they refuse, though Linda pursues with cookie in hand. Kate, a pragmatist at age four, says: "Forget it, sheep."

We all leave, the McGregors to return to Pullman, Louis and I to Tacoma. Our route cross-sections Washington's geography: vast plateau, river artery, mountains, forest-lands, inland waterway. Enchanting variety.

Right: Grain elevators form the skyline of the tiny town of St. John in the heart of the Palouse Hills wheat country.

■ *Left:* North Head Lighthouse was built in 1898 because of ship-wrecks at nearby Long Beach. ■ *Above:* Western sandpipers doze after feeding at Bowerman Basin mudflats near Hoquiam. A million shorebirds stop each spring en route from Latin America to Alaska.

■ *Above:* In 1850, San Juan Island's Roche Harbor held a Hudson's Bay Company trading post; in 1890, the West's largest lime operation. ■ *Right:* The water is fifty fathoms deep between Lummi Island and Orcas Island, with its 2,407-foot Mount Constitution.

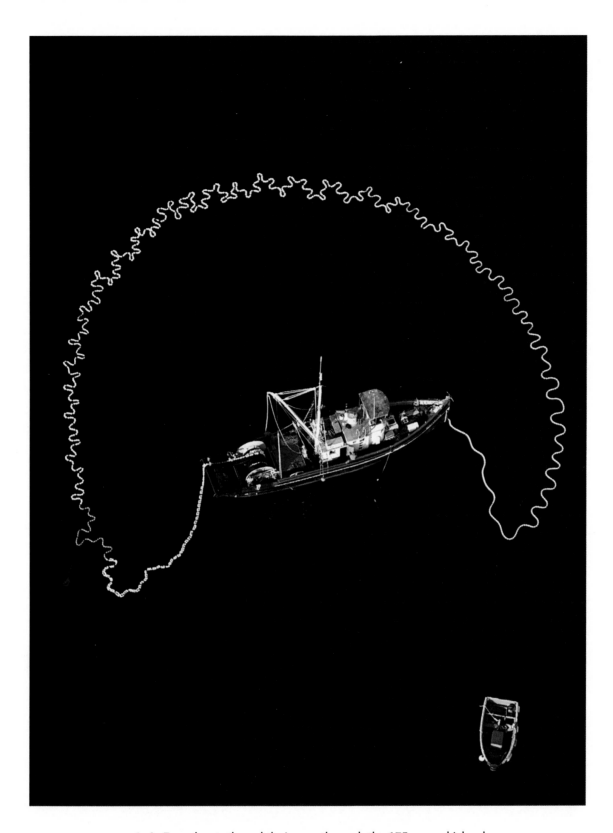

■ *Left:* Ferry boats thread their way through the 175 named islands included in the San Juans. The San Juan Islands are destinations for day trips or week-long vacations, and some lucky people live on the islands year-round. ■ *Above:* In pursuit of sockeye salmon, a purse seiner closes its eighteen-hundred-foot-long net with a winch.

■ *Left:* From Hurricane Ridge, the Olympic Mountains stand above valleys filled with early morning fog. ■ *Above:* Haro Strait has been guarded by San Juan Island's Lime Kiln Lighthouse since 1919.

■ *Above:* Using tree trunks and branches as perches, moss, fern, and club moss thrive on bigleaf maple in the moist Hoh River Valley, which receives up to 140 inches of precipitation per year.
■ *Right:* The bright blooms of rhododendrun intermingle with light green needles of new growth on a young western hemlock tree.

■ *Left:* Red heather and mountain hemlock trees in the Olympic Mountains are softened by summer fog. ■ *Above:* The Dungeness River surges through a canyon in the Jupiter Hills of the Olympic Mountains. Lieutenant Joseph P. O'Neil and his men and mules came near here in 1885. Before then, the interior of the Olympics was unknown, and O'Neil hoped to find mineral wealth there.

■ *Above:* The Columbian white-tailed deer, once abundant, has become an endangered species due to loss of suitable habitat.
■ *Right:* Willapa Bay has exported oysters since the 1850s gold rush when they were transported by schooner to San Francisco.

■ *Left:* At Point of the Arches south of Cape Flattery, sea stacks stand above slabs of upturned sedimentary rock. ■ *Above:* Bright spring Chinook salmon are a favorite delicacy in Northwest cuisine.

■ *Above:* Seeds planted near the end of May yield pumpkins in October on a farm northwest of Centralia. Along with sunny, mild summer weather, clay loam soil deposited by the Chehalis River provides good growing conditions for cucumbers, green beans, carrots, peas, sweet corn, cauliflower, broccoli, and pumpkins.

■ *Above:* The Roman-Doric legislative building, completed in 1928, dominates Olympia's skyline. Under its dome, 185 feet above the marble floors, hangs a massive brass Tiffany chandelier. Encompassing fifty-five acres, the grounds host a wide variety of flowers.

■ *Left:* Rows of ornamental cherry trees embellish the grounds of the University of Washington. Founded in 1861, the University was moved in 1895 to its present site. ■ *Above:* Built for the 1962 Seattle World's Fair, the 605-foot Space Needle is the city's most famous landmark. ■ *Overleaf:* Home to half a million, Seattle is the most northerly major city in the lower forty-eight states.

■ *Left:* Starting in the early 1900s, bulb growing has flourished in the sandy loam soils of western Washington's valleys; surprisingly, some are even exported to Holland. ■ *Above:* A pea field blooms in the Skagit Valley near Mount Vernon. Cauliflower, potatoes, cabbages, various flower bulbs, and blueberries are also grown.

■ *Above:* At 12,176 feet, Mount Adams is Washington's second-highest peak. Because of its broad shape, Mount Adams is thought to have been built by several volcanoes in close proximity. ■ *Right:* Water from the springs around Mount Adams plunges over the Upper Falls of Lewis River in Gifford Pinchot National Forest.

■ *Left:* The May 1980 eruption reduced 9,677-foot Mount St. Helens to its present height of 8,366 feet. ■ *Above:* The peaks of Goat Rocks Wilderness form the backbone of the Cascades, separating the Tieton and Klickitat river drainages on the east from the Cowlitz drainage on the west. Mount Rainier is seventy miles away.

■ *Above:* Indicating a steady stream flow and an absence of floods, lush moss grows at Twin Falls Creek between Trout Lake and Randle in the Gifford Pinchot National Forest. Glacial water from Mount Adams, traveling beneath lava flows, is the source of many streams in the area. ■ *Right:* Evidence of a volcanic history, hexagonal columns of andesite lava are found at Mount Rainier National Park.

■ *Left:* Top Lake, north of Stevens Pass, is a stop on the Pacific Crest Trail, which runs from Canada to Mexico. ■ *Above:* Goat Flats, at 4,700 feet, is part of the uplift of the Cascade Range, which began ten million years ago. Fourteen thousand years ago, glaciers carved out the Puget Sound region west of the Cascades. On clear days, Orcas Island is visible sixty miles northwest of Goat Flats.

■ *Above:* Leprechaun Lake, one of the Enchantment Lakes in the eastern Cascades, exemplifies the "enchantment" part of the name, especially when the larch turns yellow. ■ *Right:* Water droplets catch on tiny hairs on lupine leaves — a common Washington plant.

■ *Left:* In the Glacier Peak Wilderness, 6,400-foot Little Giant Pass gives hikers access to the Napeequa River. ■ *Above:* Spectacle Lake fills a depression scoured in granite by a glacier in the Cle Elum River headwaters. It is one of seven hundred lakes in the Alpine Lakes Wilderness east of Seattle. ■ *Overleaf:* East of Marblemount in North Cascades National Park, Eldorado Peak is 8,868 feet high.

■ *Left:* Scattered pockets of old-growth forest still remain in places untouched by fires or saws. ■ *Above:* Unlike neighboring Mount Baker, Mount Shuksan, at 9,127 feet high, is not volcanic in origin.

■ *Above:* Morning and evening sunlight often creates pink highlights, called alpenglow, on 10,778-foot Mount Baker. A sleeping giant, Mount Baker has erupted several times since the last Ice Age. ■ *Right:* Of Washington's volcanic giants, 10,436-foot Glacier Peak is considered the least likely to erupt in the near future.

■ *Left:* Although it is more common on the western slopes of the Cascades, here, vine maple adds a splash of color to a ponderosa pine stand on the eastern slope. ■ *Above:* Lake Chelan, fifty-one miles long and 1,529 feet deep, fills a glacier-carved valley.

■ *Above:* The Wenatchee River provides irrigation water for a fruit industry, which began in 1901 with rail shipment of apples from Wenatchee. ■ *Right:* Thirty million trees in eastern Washington supply half the nation's fresh apples, plus exports to countries as diverse as Hong Kong and Saudi Arabia. Another seven million trees grow apricots, cherries, nectarines, peaches, pears, and plums.

■ *Left:* An Indian pictograph above the Columbia River at Wishram recalls generations of Native people. ■ *Above:* On the Klickitat River, members of the Yakima Indian Nation carry on an ancient tradition of dip netting for salmon. ■ *Overleaf:* During winter low flow, snow covers cobbles of the Wenatchee River where whitefish and steelhead lurk under the surface—food for eagles and otter.

■ *Left:* The Columbia Plateau of eastern Washington was shaped first by lava flows, then by Ice Age floods, and finally by agriculture. Precipitation in some areas averages a mere seven inches, making dryland farming the rule except in the central basin. ■ *Above:* Ten to twelve inches of precipitation in the area around Waterville results in a yield of thirty to forty bushels of wheat per acre.

■ *Above:* As an erosion control measure west of Spokane, strips of wheat alternate with fallow ground. ■ *Right:* Arrowleaf balsam-root and lupine grow in the botanically rich Columbia River Gorge.

■ *Above:* Built in 1905, this Methodist church stands alone, its parishioners seemingly wheat fields, at Rocklyn near Davenport.
■ *Right:* The Spokane County Courthouse was erected in 1895.

■ *Left:* Even today, the tepee has both mystique and practicality.
■ *Above:* A hillside of western larch, also known as tamarack, puts on a brilliant fall display in the Colville National Forest east of the town of Republic. The needles of this conifer tree are shed annually.

■ *Above:* The Touchet River flows out of the Blue Mountains east of Walla Walla. Lava from these mountains once covered vast areas of eastern Washington. "Touchet" is an adaptation of the Indian word *tousa,* meaning "curing salmon before a fire." ■ *Right:* In the southeast corner of Washington, the Grande Ronde River flows through a two-thousand-foot-deep canyon cut through layers of lava rock.

■ *Above:* Four thousand square miles of Palouse Hills spread out below Steptoe Butte near the Idaho border. Windblown soil, called *loess,* along with twenty inches of precipitation, results in wheat yields of sixty to one hundred bushels per acre. Palouse Indians, in 1857, defeated Lieutenant Colonel Edward Steptoe near here.